SaNTA'S LITTLE HELPER ChRIsTMaS PlANNeR and ORgANizER

NolA LEE KeLSEy

Soggy Nomad Press
514 AMERICAS WAY
STE: 17697
BOX ELDER, SD 57719

© 2022 Soggy Nomad Press

All rights reserved. No part of this publication may be reproduced, stored in a retrieval system or transmitted in any form or by any means, electronic, mechanical, recording or otherwise without the prior written permission from the publisher.

ISBN: 978-1-957532-01-1

Cover design by Nola Lee Kelsey

This Planner Belongs to:

_____

_____

Christmas Bucket List

No.	Activity	Date	Done
			☐
			☐
			☐
			☐
			☐
			☐
			☐
			☐
			☐
			☐
			☐
			☐
			☐
			☐
			☐
			☐
			☐
			☐
			☐
			☐
			☐
			☐
			☐
			☐
			☐
			☐

Christmas Bucket List

No.	Activity	Date	Done
			☐
			☐
			☐
			☐
			☐
			☐
			☐
			☐
			☐
			☐
			☐
			☐
			☐
			☐
			☐
			☐
			☐
			☐
			☐
			☐
			☐
			☐
			☐
			☐
			☐
			☐

No.	Activity	Date	Done
			☐
			☐
			☐
			☐
			☐
			☐
			☐
			☐
			☐
			☐
			☐
			☐
			☐
			☐
			☐
			☐
			☐
			☐
			☐
			☐
			☐
			☐
			☐
			☐
			☐
			☐

No.	Activity	Date	Done
			☐
			☐
			☐
			☐
			☐
			☐
			☐
			☐
			☐
			☐
			☐
			☐
			☐
			☐
			☐
			☐
			☐
			☐
			☐
			☐
			☐
			☐
			☐
			☐
			☐
			☐

No.	Task Description	Done
		☐
		☐
		☐
		☐
		☐
		☐
		☐
		☐
		☐
		☐
		☐
		☐
		☐
		☐
		☐
		☐
		☐
		☐
		☐
		☐
		☐
		☐
		☐
		☐
		☐
		☐

No.	Task Description	Done
		☐
		☐
		☐
		☐
		☐
		☐
		☐
		☐
		☐
		☐
		☐
		☐
		☐
		☐
		☐
		☐
		☐
		☐
		☐
		☐
		☐
		☐
		☐
		☐
		☐
		☐

No.	Task Description	Done
		☐
		☐
		☐
		☐
		☐
		☐
		☐
		☐
		☐
		☐
		☐
		☐
		☐
		☐
		☐
		☐
		☐
		☐
		☐
		☐
		☐
		☐
		☐
		☐
		☐
		☐

No.	Task Description	Done
		☐
		☐
		☐
		☐
		☐
		☐
		☐
		☐
		☐
		☐
		☐
		☐
		☐
		☐
		☐
		☐
		☐
		☐
		☐
		☐
		☐
		☐
		☐
		☐
		☐
		☐

Gift Idea Tracker

GIFT FOR	ITEM NAME	STORE NAME / WEBSITE	PRICE

Gift Idea Tracker

GIFT FOR	ITEM NAME	STORE NAME / WEBSITE	PRICE

GIFT FOR	ITEM NAME	STORE NAME / WEBSITE	PRICE

GIFT FOR	ITEM NAME	STORE NAME / WEBSITE	PRICE

Online Shopping TRACKING

ITEM	STORE NAME / WEBSITE	COST	ORDER DATE	SHIP DATE	GOT
					☐
					☐
					☐
					☐
					☐
					☐
					☐
					☐
					☐
					☐
					☐
					☐
					☐
					☐
					☐
					☐
					☐
					☐
					☐
					☐
					☐
					☐
					☐
					☐
					☐
					☐

Online Shopping TRACKING

ITEM	STORE NAME / WEBSITE	COST	ORDER DATE	SHIP DATE	GOT
					☐
					☐
					☐
					☐
					☐
					☐
					☐
					☐
					☐
					☐
					☐
					☐
					☐
					☐
					☐
					☐
					☐
					☐
					☐
					☐
					☐
					☐
					☐
					☐
					☐
					☐

Online Shopping TRACKING

ITEM	STORE NAME / WEBSITE	COST	ORDER DATE	SHIP DATE	GOT
					☐
					☐
					☐
					☐
					☐
					☐
					☐
					☐
					☐
					☐
					☐
					☐
					☐
					☐
					☐
					☐
					☐
					☐
					☐
					☐
					☐
					☐
					☐
					☐
					☐
					☐
					☐
					☐

Online Shopping TRACKING

ITEM	STORE NAME / WEBSITE	COST	ORDER DATE	SHIP DATE	GOT
					☐
					☐
					☐
					☐
					☐
					☐
					☐
					☐
					☐
					☐
					☐
					☐
					☐
					☐
					☐
					☐
					☐
					☐
					☐
					☐
					☐
					☐
					☐
					☐
					☐
					☐

Name:		Budget:	Wrapped: ☐ Received: ☐
Item	Description	Store/Website	Price
			Total:

Name:		Budget:	Wrapped: ☐ Received: ☐
Item	Description	Store/Website	Price
			Total:

Gift Giving Tracker

Name:		Budget:	Wrapped: ☐ Received: ☐
Item	Description	Store/Website	Price
			Total:

Name:		Budget:	Wrapped: ☐ Received: ☐
Item	Description	Store/Website	Price
			Total:

 # Gift Giving TRACKER

Name:		Budget:	Wrapped: ☐ Received: ☐
Item	Description	Store/Website	Price
			Total:

Name:		Budget:	Wrapped: ☐ Received: ☐
Item	Description	Store/Website	Price
			Total:

Gift Giving Tracker

Name: | Budget: | Wrapped: ☐ Received: ☐

Item	Description	Store/Website	Price
		Total:	

Name: | Budget: | Wrapped: ☐ Received: ☐

Item	Description	Store/Website	Price
		Total:	

Name:		Budget:	Wrapped: ☐ Received: ☐
Item	Description	Store/Website	Price
		Total:	

Name:		Budget:	Wrapped: ☐ Received: ☐
Item	Description	Store/Website	Price
		Total:	

Gift Giving Tracker

Name: _____ Budget: _____ Wrapped: ☐ Received: ☐

Item	Description	Store/Website	Price
		Total:	

Name: _____ Budget: _____ Wrapped: ☐ Received: ☐

Item	Description	Store/Website	Price
		Total:	

 # Gift Giving
TRACKER

Name:		Budget:	Wrapped: ☐ Received: ☐
Item	**Description**	**Store/Website**	**Price**
			Total:

Name:		Budget:	Wrapped: ☐ Received: ☐
Item	**Description**	**Store/Website**	**Price**
			Total:

Gift Giving TRACKER

Name:		Budget:	Wrapped: ☐ Received: ☐
Item	Description	Store/Website	Price
		Total:	

Name:		Budget:	Wrapped: ☐ Received: ☐
Item	Description	Store/Website	Price
		Total:	

Name:		Budget:	Wrapped: ☐ Received: ☐
Item	Description	Store/Website	Price
			Total:

Name:		Budget:	Wrapped: ☐ Received: ☐
Item	Description	Store/Website	Price
			Total:

Gift Giving Tracker

Name: _____ Budget: _____ Wrapped: ☐ Received: ☐

Item	Description	Store/Website	Price
		Total:	

Name: _____ Budget: _____ Wrapped: ☐ Received: ☐

Item	Description	Store/Website	Price
		Total:	

 # Gift Giving TRACKER

Name:		Budget:	Wrapped: ☐ Received: ☐
Item	Description	Store/Website	Price
			Total:

Name:		Budget:	Wrapped: ☐ Received: ☐
Item	Description	Store/Website	Price
			Total:

 # Gift Giving TRACKER

Name:		Budget:	Wrapped: ☐ Received: ☐
Item	Description	Store/Website	Price
			Total:

Name:		Budget:	Wrapped: ☐ Received: ☐
Item	Description	Store/Website	Price
			Total:

Name:		Budget:	Wrapped: ☐ Received: ☐
Item	Description	Store/Website	Price
		Total:	

Name:		Budget:	Wrapped: ☐ Received: ☐
Item	Description	Store/Website	Price
		Total:	

Name:		Budget:	Wrapped: ☐ Received: ☐
Item	Description	Store/Website	Price
		Total:	

Name:		Budget:	Wrapped: ☐ Received: ☐
Item	Description	Store/Website	Price
		Total:	

Stocking Stuffer IDEAS

Name:

Stocking Stuffer Idea	Store/Website	Price
1.		
2.		
3.		
4.		
5.		
6.		
7.		
8.		
9.		
10.		
	Total:	

Name:

Stocking Stuffer Idea	Store/Website	Price
1.		
2.		
3.		
4.		
5.		
6.		
7.		
8.		
9.		
10.		
	Total:	

 # Stocking Stuffer IDEAS

Name:

	Stocking Stuffer Idea	Store/Website	Price
1.			
2.			
3.			
4.			
5.			
6.			
7.			
8.			
9.			
10.			Total:

Name:

	Stocking Stuffer Idea	Store/Website	Price
1.			
2.			
3.			
4.			
5.			
6.			
7.			
8.			
9.			
10.			Total:

Stocking Stuffer IDEAS

Name:

	Stocking Stuffer Idea	Store/Website	Price
1.			
2.			
3.			
4.			
5.			
6.			
7.			
8.			
9.			
10.			
		Total:	

Name:

	Stocking Stuffer Idea	Store/Website	Price
1.			
2.			
3.			
4.			
5.			
6.			
7.			
8.			
9.			
10.			
		Total:	

Stocking Stuffer IDEAS

Name:

	Stocking Stuffer Idea	Store/Website	Price
1.			
2.			
3.			
4.			
5.			
6.			
7.			
8.			
9.			
10.			
		Total:	

Name:

	Stocking Stuffer Idea	Store/Website	Price
1.			
2.			
3.			
4.			
5.			
6.			
7.			
8.			
9.			
10.			
		Total:	

Stocking Stuffer IDEAS

Name:

	Stocking Stuffer Idea	Store/Website	Price
1.			
2.			
3.			
4.			
5.			
6.			
7.			
8.			
9.			
10.			
		Total:	

Name:

	Stocking Stuffer Idea	Store/Website	Price
1.			
2.			
3.			
4.			
5.			
6.			
7.			
8.			
9.			
10.			
		Total:	

 # Stocking Stuffer IDEAS

Name:

	Stocking Stuffer Idea	Store/Website	Price
1.			
2.			
3.			
4.			
5.			
6.			
7.			
8.			
9.			
10.			
		Total:	

Name:

	Stocking Stuffer Idea	Store/Website	Price
1.			
2.			
3.			
4.			
5.			
6.			
7.			
8.			
9.			
10.			
		Total:	

 # Stocking Stuffer IDEAS

Name:

	Stocking Stuffer Idea	Store/Website	Price
1.			
2.			
3.			
4.			
5.			
6.			
7.			
8.			
9.			
10.			
		Total:	

Name:

	Stocking Stuffer Idea	Store/Website	Price
1.			
2.			
3.			
4.			
5.			
6.			
7.			
8.			
9.			
10.			
		Total:	

Stocking Stuffer IDEAS

Name:

	Stocking Stuffer Idea	Store/Website	Price
1.			
2.			
3.			
4.			
5.			
6.			
7.			
8.			
9.			
10.			
		Total:	

Name:

	Stocking Stuffer Idea	Store/Website	Price
1.			
2.			
3.			
4.			
5.			
6.			
7.			
8.			
9.			
10.			
		Total:	

Christmas Card TRACKER

Name:
Email:
Address

Message

Sent: ☐ Received: ☐

Name:
Email:
Address

Message

Sent: ☐ Received: ☐

Name:
Email:
Address

Message

Sent: ☐ Received: ☐

Name:
Email:
Address

Message

Sent: ☐ Received: ☐

Christmas Card Tracker

Name:
Email:
Address

Message

Sent: ☐ Received: ☐

Name:
Email:
Address

Message

Sent: ☐ Received: ☐

Name:
Email:
Address

Message

Sent: ☐ Received: ☐

Name:
Email:
Address

Message

Sent: ☐ Received: ☐

Christmas Card TRACKER

Name:
Email:

Address

Message

Sent: ☐ Received: ☐

Name:
Email:

Address

Message

Sent: ☐ Received: ☐

Name:
Email:

Address

Message

Sent: ☐ Received: ☐

Name:
Email:

Address

Message

Sent: ☐ Received: ☐

Christmas Card Tracker

Name:
Email:
Address

Message

Sent: ☐ Received: ☐

Name:
Email:
Address

Message

Sent: ☐ Received: ☐

Name:
Email:
Address

Message

Sent: ☐ Received: ☐

Name:
Email:
Address

Message

Sent: ☐ Received: ☐

Christmas Card Tracker

Name:
Email:

Address

Message

Sent: ☐ Received: ☐

Name:
Email:

Address

Message

Sent: ☐ Received: ☐

Name:
Email:

Address

Message

Sent: ☐ Received: ☐

Name:
Email:

Address

Message

Sent: ☐ Received: ☐

Christmas Card TRACKER

Name:	Name:
Email:	Email:

Address

Message

Sent: ☐ Received: ☐

Address

Message

Sent: ☐ Received: ☐

Name:	Name:
Email:	Email:

Address

Message

Sent: ☐ Received: ☐

Address

Message

Sent: ☐ Received: ☐

Christmas Card TRACKER

Name:
Email:
Address

Message

Sent: ☐ Received: ☐

Name:
Email:
Address

Message

Sent: ☐ Received: ☐

Name:
Email:
Address

Message

Sent: ☐ Received: ☐

Name:
Email:
Address

Message

Sent: ☐ Received: ☐

Christmas Card Tracker

Name:
Email:
Address

Message

Sent: ☐ Received: ☐

Name:
Email:
Address

Message

Sent: ☐ Received: ☐

Name:
Email:
Address

Message

Sent: ☐ Received: ☐

Name:
Email:
Address

Message

Sent: ☐ Received: ☐

Christmas Card TRACKER

Name:
Email:

Address

_____
_____
_____
_____

Message

_____
_____
_____
_____

Sent: ☐   Received: ☐

Name:
Email:

Address

_____
_____
_____
_____

Message

_____
_____
_____
_____

Sent: ☐   Received: ☐

Name:
Email:

Address

_____
_____
_____
_____

Message

_____
_____
_____
_____

Sent: ☐   Received: ☐

Name:
Email:

Address

_____
_____
_____
_____

Message

_____
_____
_____
_____

Sent: ☐   Received: ☐

Christmas Card TRACKER

Name:
Email:
Address

Message

Sent: ☐ Received: ☐

Name:
Email:
Address

Message

Sent: ☐ Received: ☐

Name:
Email:
Address

Message

Sent: ☐ Received: ☐

Name:
Email:
Address

Message

Sent: ☐ Received: ☐

Christmas Card TRACKER

Name:
Email:
Address

Message

Sent: ☐ Received: ☐

Name:
Email:
Address

Message

Sent: ☐ Received: ☐

Name:
Email:
Address

Message

Sent: ☐ Received: ☐

Name:
Email:
Address

Message

Sent: ☐ Received: ☐

Christmas Card Tracker

Entry 1
- Name:
- Email:
- Address
- Message
- Sent: ☐ Received: ☐

Entry 2
- Name:
- Email:
- Address
- Message
- Sent: ☐ Received: ☐

Entry 3
- Name:
- Email:
- Address
- Message
- Sent: ☐ Received: ☐

Entry 4
- Name:
- Email:
- Address
- Message
- Sent: ☐ Received: ☐

Christmas Card Tracker

Name:
Email:
Address

Message

Sent: ☐ Received: ☐

Name:
Email:
Address

Message

Sent: ☐ Received: ☐

Name:
Email:
Address

Message

Sent: ☐ Received: ☐

Name:
Email:
Address

Message

Sent: ☐ Received: ☐

Christmas Card Tracker

Name:
Email:
Address

Message

Sent: ☐ Received: ☐

Name:
Email:
Address

Message

Sent: ☐ Received: ☐

Name:
Email:
Address

Message

Sent: ☐ Received: ☐

Name:
Email:
Address

Message

Sent: ☐ Received: ☐

Christmas Card Tracker

Name:
Email:
Address

Message

Sent: ☐ Received: ☐

Name:
Email:
Address

Message

Sent: ☐ Received: ☐

Name:
Email:
Address

Message

Sent: ☐ Received: ☐

Name:
Email:
Address

Message

Sent: ☐ Received: ☐

Christmas Card TRACKER

Name:
Email:
Address

Message

Sent: ☐ Received: ☐

Name:
Email:
Address

Message

Sent: ☐ Received: ☐

Name:
Email:
Address

Message

Sent: ☐ Received: ☐

Name:
Email:
Address

Message

Sent: ☐ Received: ☐

Room	Theme	Color Scheme

Items to Buy	#/Color/Size	Place to Purchase

Room	Theme	Color Scheme

Items to Buy	#/Color/Size	Place to Purchase

Room	Theme	Color Scheme

Items to Buy	#/Color/Size	Place to Purchase

Room	Theme	Color Scheme

Items to Buy	#/Color/Size	Place to Purchase

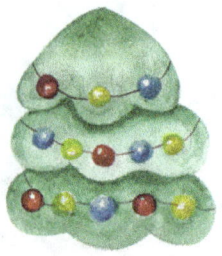  

Decoration PLANNING

Room	Theme	Color Scheme

Items to Buy	#/Color/Size	Place to Purchase

Room	Theme	Color Scheme

Items to Buy	#/Color/Size	Place to Purchase

Room	Theme	Color Scheme

Items to Buy	#/Color/Size	Place to Purchase

Room	Theme	Color Scheme

Items to Buy	#/Color/Size	Place to Purchase

Decoration PLANNING

Room	Theme	Color Scheme

Items to Buy	#/Color/Size	Place to Purchase

Room	Theme	Color Scheme

Items to Buy	#/Color/Size	Place to Purchase

Decoration PLANNING

Room	Theme	Color Scheme

Items to Buy	#/Color/Size	Place to Purchase

Room	Theme	Color Scheme

Items to Buy	#/Color/Size	Place to Purchase

Decoration PLANNING

Room	Theme	Color Scheme

Items to Buy	#/Color/Size	Place to Purchase

Room	Theme	Color Scheme

Items to Buy	#/Color/Size	Place to Purchase

Decoration Planning

Room	Theme	Color Scheme

Items to Buy	#/Color/Size	Place to Purchase

Room	Theme	Color Scheme

Items to Buy	#/Color/Size	Place to Purchase

Decoration INVENTORY

DINING ROOM

Item	QTY.	Location
1.		
2.		
3.		
4.		
5.		
6.		
7.		
8.		
9.		
10.		

LIVING ROOM

Item	QTY.	Location
1.		
2.		
3.		
4.		
5.		
6.		
7.		
8.		
9.		
10.		

Decoration INVENTORY

BEDROOM #1

Item	QTY.	Location
1.		
2.		
3.		
4.		
5.		
6.		
7.		
8.		
9.		
10.		

BEDROOM #2

Item	QTY.	Location
1.		
2.		
3.		
4.		
5.		
6.		
7.		
8.		
9.		
10.		

Decoration INVENTORY

BATHROOM #1		
Item	QTY.	Location
1.		
2.		
3.		
4.		
5.		
6.		
7.		
8.		
9.		
10.		

BATHROOM #2		
Item	QTY.	Location
1.		
2.		
3.		
4.		
5.		
6.		
7.		
8.		
9.		
10.		

Party Planning IDEAS

Date _____ **Time** _____ **Venue** _____

DECORATIONS

GAMES/ACTIVITES

SONG LIST

ENTERTAINMENT

Party Planning IDEAS

Date _____ Time _____ Venue _____

DECORATIONS	GAMES/ACTIVITES

SONG LIST	ENTERTAINMENT

Party Planning Ideas

Date _____ Time _____ Venue _____

DECORATIONS	GAMES/ACTIVITES

SONG LIST	ENTERTAINMENT

Guest Name	No. of Guests	Dietary Notes	RSVP'd
			☐
			☐
			☐
			☐
			☐
			☐
			☐
			☐
			☐
			☐
			☐
			☐
			☐
			☐
			☐
			☐
			☐
			☐
			☐
			☐
			☐
			☐
			☐
			☐
			☐
			☐
			☐

Guest Name	No. of Guests	Dietary Notes	RSVP'd
			☐
			☐
			☐
			☐
			☐
			☐
			☐
			☐
			☐
			☐
			☐
			☐
			☐
			☐
			☐
			☐
			☐
			☐
			☐
			☐
			☐
			☐
			☐
			☐
			☐

 # Party Guest List

Guest Name	No. of Guests	Dietary Notes	RSVP'd
			☐
			☐
			☐
			☐
			☐
			☐
			☐
			☐
			☐
			☐
			☐
			☐
			☐
			☐
			☐
			☐
			☐
			☐
			☐
			☐
			☐
			☐
			☐
			☐
			☐
			☐

Party Guest List

Guest Name	No. of Guests	Dietary Notes	RSVP'd
			☐
			☐
			☐
			☐
			☐
			☐
			☐
			☐
			☐
			☐
			☐
			☐
			☐
			☐
			☐
			☐
			☐
			☐
			☐
			☐
			☐
			☐
			☐
			☐
			☐

Holiday Recipe

Recipe Name: _____

Servings	Prep Time	Cook Time	Oven Temp

Size	Ingredients	Directions

Notes: _____

 # Holiday Recipe

Recipe Name: _____

Servings	Prep Time	Cook Time	Oven Temp

Size	Ingredients	Directions

Notes: _____

 # Holiday Recipe

Recipe Name: _____

Servings	Prep Time	Cook Time	Oven Temp

Size	Ingredients	Directions

Notes: _____

 # Holiday Recipe

Recipe Name: _____

Servings	Prep Time	Cook Time	Oven Temp

Size	Ingredients	Directions

Notes: _____

 # Holiday Recipe

Recipe Name: _____

Servings	Prep Time	Cook Time	Oven Temp

Size	Ingredients	Directions

Notes: _____

 # Holiday Recipe

Recipe Name: _____

Servings	Prep Time	Cook Time	Oven Temp

Size	Ingredients	Directions	

Notes: _____

 # Holiday Recipe

Recipe Name: _____

Servings	Prep Time	Cook Time	Oven Temp

Size	Ingredients	Directions

Notes: _____

 # Holiday Recipe

Recipe Name: _____

Servings	Prep Time	Cook Time	Oven Temp

Size	Ingredients	Directions

Notes: _____

 # Holiday Recipe

Recipe Name: _____

Servings	Prep Time	Cook Time	Oven Temp

Size	Ingredients	Directions

Notes: _____

Holiday Recipe

Recipe Name: _____

Servings	Prep Time	Cook Time	Oven Temp

Size	Ingredients	Directions

Notes: _____

Holiday Recipe

Recipe Name: _____

Servings	Prep Time	Cook Time	Oven Temp

Size	Ingredients	Directions

Notes: _____

Holiday Recipe

Recipe Name: _____

Servings	Prep Time	Cook Time	Oven Temp

Size	Ingredients	Directions

Notes: _____

Holiday Meal Planner

BREAKFAST

LUNCH

DINNER

SHOPPING LIST

 # Holiday Meal PLANNER

BREAKFAST

LUNCH

DINNER

SHOPPING LIST

 # Holiday Meal PLANNER

BREAKFAST

LUNCH

DINNER

SHOPPING LIST

Holiday Meal Planner

BREAKFAST

LUNCH

DINNER

SHOPPING LIST

Holiday Meal PLANNER

BREAKFAST

LUNCH

DINNER

SHOPPING LIST

 # Holiday Meal PLANNER

BREAKFAST

LUNCH

DINNER

SHOPPING LIST

 # Holiday Meal PLANNER

BREAKFAST

LUNCH

DINNER

SHOPPING LIST

Holiday Meal Planner

BREAKFAST

LUNCH

DINNER

SHOPPING LIST

 # Holiday Meal PLANNER

BREAKFAST

LUNCH

DINNER

SHOPPING LIST

 # Holiday Meal PLANNER

BREAKFAST

LUNCH

DINNER

SHOPPING LIST

Notes

Notes

Notes

Notes

Notes

Notes

Notes

Notes

Notes

Notes

Notes

Notes

Notes

Notes

Notes

Notes

Notes

Notes

Notes

Notes

Notes

www.ingramcontent.com/pod-product-compliance
Lightning Source LLC
Chambersburg PA
CBHW081310070526
44578CB00006B/828